GU00866327

First published in 2018
Copyright © William Lane 2018

All rights reserved. Save for private individual study purposes not for monetary gain, no part of this book may be reproduced or transmitted in any form or by any means, electronic or mechanical, including photocopying, recording, or by any information storage and retrieval system, without permission in writing from the author.

The Scripture quotations contained herein are from The New Revised Standard Version of the Bible, Anglicized Edition, copyright © 1989, 1995 by the Division of Christian Education of the National Council of the Churches of Christ in the United States of America, and are used by permission. All Rights Reserved.

The quotation from *Undersong*, by Peter Price, published and copyright © 2002 by Darton Longman and Todd Ltd, London, is used by permission of the publishers.

ISBN-13: 978-1981806072
ISBN-10: 1981806075

Typeset in Times New Roman

Dedicated to my brother, John

1953-2005

CONTENTS

Introduction

For most of us our particular God-view is an accident of birth. For the vast majority of people the particular story which prevails at the place, time and culture of their birth is the story they adopt, or at least know something about and at some level tend towards. For them the stories of other places and cultures are "other".

My story is the Christian story because I was born in England to a conventional, Christian (in the traditional English sense) family. If I had been born in Baghdad my story would almost certainly be the Moslem story. If I had been born in Chennai my story would almost certainly be the Hindu story.

What follows does not attempt to be an academic, theological treatise. What follows is an offering of a way of looking at and thinking through matters of Christian faith and spirituality which might be new, challenging and helpful to some who, like me, ponder and ponder over things and who find certainty, absolute truth, dogma, doctrine and exclusive claims, to be very hard to accept.

I hope I may have gone some way towards uncovering a Higher Power, a God, to whom we can relate, who makes at least some sense to us, and whom we both can and want to contemplate, worship and communicate with as the author and sustainer of life. Faith is never static; it is a continuous journey of stopping and starting, of discovering and rejecting and accepting. Faith is not there as some abstract part of life just for its own sake. It would be futile and pointless if it were. Faith is there because it feeds our sense of being and worth, bringing shape and direction, point and purpose and, hopefully, joy to our relationships and to our whole lives.

In recent times I have come across an ancient poem attributed to Kalidasa, an Indian Sanskrit playwright and poet. The poem has struck me very much because it touches upon so much of how I have come to understand things of God. It has provided me with a loose framework for what follows.

Look to this day,

For it is life,

The very life of life.

In its brief course lie all

The realities and verities of existence,

The bliss of growth,

The splendour of action,

The glory of power –

For yesterday is but a dream

And tomorrow only a vision,

But this day, well lived,

Makes every yesterday a dream of happiness

And every tomorrow a vision of hope.

Look well, therefore, to this day.[1]

Chapter One

Shifting Sands – A Little Bit of My Story

My journey so far convinces me that our spiritual faith and understanding, whatever religion may be ours, is not static, is never complete, is forever shifting and changing; it is a journey with no definite and final destination that we shall ever know, at least not in this mortal life.

My journey began with a childhood enjoyment and acceptance of the conventional Christian story I was taught at school and occasionally at Sunday school. This extraordinary story was fascinating, exciting and somehow seemed to me to be profoundly important. It touched me deep within.

In teenage years this developed during my time at a boarding school which had deep Anglican roots and at which Christian principles and precepts ran like a golden thread through school life. Daily chapel worship was all part of the rhythm of life: compulsory Book of Common Prayer Evensong, and sung Holy Communion on Sundays. I loved it all and soon became deeply involved: choir member, regular robed server, bell ringer and even one time secretary of a weekly Bible reading and discussion group called "Christian Forum". It was only much later in life that I realised this group was something of a breakaway group – the evangelicals doing "proper" Christianity alongside, or maybe as an antidote to, the high Anglican stuff that was the school's default.

And so I left that place a committed, confirmed Christian. Until fairly recently, if some well-meaning person had asked me when I became a Christian, I would have said 'Then, in my teens, at that boarding school'. My answer now would be very different; it would be less precise, ambivalent, uncertain and therefore, for many, rather unsatisfactory. The whys and wherefores are very much part of the exploration of this small book.

In my early twenties, enjoying young love with the person whom I would go on to marry, and exploring life loosed from the ties of home and school, I didn't attend much to my faith. It was there, but very much "on the back burner". It was really as marriage and then children came along that matters of faith began to become important for me again, and this time – not as a conscious decision but rather through the encouragement and invitations of friends – I found myself in a growing, lively, very contemporary, charismatic evangelical church on an Alpha Course;[2] and for the next few years that was my lot. I owe a very great deal to that church, to those people and to the Alpha Course. I got to know the Bible reasonably well, I learned the Christian doctrines and dogmas and thought I was getting to know and believe the right things - the truths and certainties of the Christian faith. I developed a relationship with God rather than simply having some knowledge about God. I got to attend all sorts of exciting conferences and camps. I had some profound and very real spiritual experiences - all good stuff which re-awakened a long-held sense of calling to ordained ministry. I looked forward to training at an evangelical theological college, followed then by ordination and a curacy[3] at a lively evangelical church, followed by a life of ministry proclaiming and preaching an exclusive gospel of salvation through faith in Jesus Christ in the power of the Holy Spirit.

And then everything began to change. I can't put my finger on any one thing, and maybe the change was going to happen anyway, whatever else may or may not have happened. Maybe it was my mind, my spirit, my soul that was on the move, perhaps nudged along by events, people and places.

I was in my thirties and I began to become close to my brother who was ten years older than me. He lived much of his life in South East India running some health and education projects in a very underdeveloped area. He had become a complete Indophile – steeped in the culture and in love with the people and place, almost obsessed. It was through his experience of life among the largely Roman Catholic community (within a deeply Hindu culture and context) in that corner of India that my brother formally converted to Roman Catholicism.

I began to spend much time with him when he was in England and we often chewed the cud very late into the night on all matters church and spiritual. My brother was politically, socially and theologically liberal. In the early days we often disagreed. I remember him asking me one time, in the course of one of those late night conversations, 'So are you saying that anyone who doesn't accept Jesus as their Lord and saviour, and who doesn't accept him as the one and only way to heaven, is eternally lost?' I said 'Yes', and he was shocked, perhaps somewhat offended, and certainly disappointed. His reaction was silent but very obvious. And as I gave my answer I was vaguely aware of having shocked and offended myself too!

Not long after that, I took the opportunity to spend three weeks with my brother in India as he went about his life and work. It was a remarkable experience – enough for a whole travelogue by itself. The extraordinary thing for me was experiencing a place that was culturally completely and absolutely Hindu: the temples, customs, clothes, rituals, spirituality, superstition, food, the whole mindset and worldview – completely and absolutely Hindu.

I recall one occasion when I was taken by a friendly Swami[4], who was doing an amazing job running an orphanage for abandoned and orphaned children, to a very small Hindu temple deep in the woods, which he and some of his charges had spent tireless hours caring for and elaborately re-painting. There I sat and watched as the children, led by Swami, spent time in Hindu religious ritual and prayer. I was captivated and my heart was deeply touched. The presence of the Spirit of God was palpable. I came away from that experience in no doubt whatsoever that what I had observed and experienced was a taste of the Kingdom of God – the same Kingdom and the same God we worship and speak of in our Christian tradition and, I am now convinced, in all the other mainline religious traditions, and, I have no doubt, in countless more besides.

Alongside the Hindu context and culture of South India, and fully absorbed into it, are a very significant minority of Christians – mostly Roman Catholics. It was intriguing to see Christianity being played out in a Hindu way.

The Indian Roman Catholic family with whom I spent much time was to have their newly built home blessed. On the allotted afternoon the whole family and many friends assembled not for one, but two ceremonies. First Swami arrived and carried out an elaborate ritual in which a chicken was chased and transfixed into a torpor, whereupon the mesmerised beast was set to stand, motionless, on a coconut, and a gleaming cutlass was taken and the chicken's head was swiped clean off! The blood of the hapless creature was then daubed on the door frames of the new home. Swami did lots of other things too with brightly coloured spices.

No sooner was this completed than the Parish Priest arrived from the local Catholic church. Donned in his priestly robes, he set about blessing the new home with lashings of holy water and prayers whilst the assembled crowd, including saffron-clad Swami, looked on with quiet reverence. When these formal rituals were done, everybody – priest, Swami and all – partied.

It was magnificent. Something very profound had taken place. God had been invoked and involved. The new home had been blessed – somehow drawn into a stream of holiness - blown through with benevolent, loving and protecting energy. Christian and Hindu had somehow lost all their outward differences and become one – invoking, revering and celebrating that good, loving, creative and universe-filling energy which we call "God".

Some years later I read a book by Peter Price (one time Bishop of Bath & Wells) in which he wrote of an experience in India which so reminded me of my own. This is what he wrote:

Around the Hindu festival of lights, Diwali, I visited a group of [Dalits, or "untouchables" - the lowest caste of Hindus, the lowest of the low in Indian society] *in the company of Christians who had been working for some time to help the community organize itself to enable it to obtain basic rights of sanitation, health care and food vouchers for their children. The first triumph was to obtain a standpipe and a tap - running water. This simple utility meant that the neighbourhood could be registered as a 'house', and the other benefits became possible. Mutual respect and love existed between the Christians and Hindus, and on the night of the festival we were invited to the ramshackle community of tents to share a feast.*

Our arrival was greeted in the darkened street by firecrackers. Around the tent tables and chairs had been found, places of honour set up for the principal of the local seminary and me. With great joy our hosts shared the food they had prepared. There was much laughter, though from my point of view little real understanding of the language. Our hosts did not eat with us; they watched attentively, smiling, busying themselves around us to make sure we had enough. When we asked when they would eat, they replied, 'When you have gone - then we can talk about you!' Speeches were made, the meal was over, and in the mingling that followed many tears were shed amidst the laughter and embracing. It was like a taste of heaven, where the whole of humanity has come together: those regarded as untouchable were being touched, those whose history had been one of exclusion, were being inclusive and included. [ ] Later I described this event as like 'dining in the Kingdom of God'.[5]

My time in India really made me think. What I thought were the norms of Christianity had been profoundly challenged. What I thought were truths about salvation had been challenged. What I thought was the unequivocal truth of and necessity for exclusively Christian faith had been challenged. Big questions about God, life and the universe began to loom large in my mind and in my heart. Suddenly the truths and certainties to which I had so readily subscribed began to feel as if they might not be quite so unequivocally true, not quite so certain. I was beginning to feel very uncomfortable. And so began an exciting, and at times very painful and confusing, personal spiritual journey away from certainty, absolutism, dogma, doctrine and exclusivity, towards a different spirituality and understanding – one that is fluid, shifting and liberating.

I did go on to train at an evangelical college and, following ordination, I did spend three years in a lively, evangelical church as a curate. It was whilst I was there that John, my wonderful brother, called "The Apostle of Rameswaram"[6] by some of the folk amongst whom he had lived and worked, and who had only in recent years become my best friend and spiritual soul mate, died at 52.

Now I minister in a rather different kind of place. As joys and tragedies continue to happen, my story continues to evolve and develop, to shift and to change. It is shaped by experience, by feeling, by contemplation and rumination, by occasional moments of certainty and by even more moments of painful doubt. My story is shaped by an uncontrollable and compulsive inner urge and insistence that every single human being is uniquely precious, and that any God I believe in has to be one who doesn't give special privileges to those who believe in him in one particular way rather than another, or not at all.

Chapter Two

The Realities and Verities of Existence

I sometimes ask classes of primary school children to draw God. Almost always the pictures are of men – usually old and bearded! Sometimes I am asked to field questions in a class of little ones. I have been asked some fascinating questions: Where does God live? What does God do? Why can't we see God? Why does God let bad thing happen? Is my dog in heaven? Will everyone go to heaven? Where is heaven? How do we get there when we're dead? My dad doesn't believe in God; do I have to?

I love the way children ask the direct and challenging questions that we adults often prefer to avoid. They are incredibly hard to answer in a helpful, honest and real way. Of course, there are the standard and somewhat clichéd "Christian" answers, but they really won't do. Children are not swayed by them, and nor any longer am I.

Humanity is still undergoing a revolution which began with the onset of The Enlightenment in the late 17th and 18th centuries whereby intellectuals turned to reason, rather than tradition, for their thinking about the world and about God. This new way of thinking was supplemented by the Industrial Revolution in the early 19th century when people were turning to machines for manufacture and transport, and to science in ways never before known. From that point on there was a rapid quest for discovery about the world and the universe, about the make up of things, how they work, and how so-called "defects" in nature can be remedied, particularly in the human body. So it has continued ever since.

We live in a technological world. All the digital wonders of today are not a temporary and passing fad; they are the new "normal", as normal as the very air we breathe. We can't be surprised about youngsters being welded to their smart phones and tablets whilst we wistfully hark back to the days when we climbed trees in the fresh air. Smart phones, tablets, computers, on-demand TV, cashless shopping, the internet – it's all today's normality. Things will not go back to the way they were before. They never have done. Human society, along with the whole of creation is constantly on the move – shifting, changing, "advancing". Nothing ever stays the same.

We know so much now about the structure and workings of our planet and of the universe. The discoveries of biologists, chemists, geologists, physicists and astrophysicists are mind-blowing. They know so much, and you can bet your bottom dollar that for those things that remain unknown, there are armies of white-coated clever people heading full-pelt towards the answers.

This vast accumulation of knowledge shapes our worldview both physically and spiritually. We expect things to be rationally explained. We expect answers that are logical and reasonable. We expect ideas and theories to be proved: "You show me and I'll believe it". This is why it is almost impossible to give satisfactory answers to the kinds of questions which children ask about God; and they are questions most adults want to ask too, but we somehow know that the stock answers just won't quite hit the mark.

Compare this high-tech world in which we live to the world of a few hundred years and more ago. Compare it to the world which was the biblical backdrop. There was no science (although the ancient Greeks and Egyptians were pretty hot on maths and geometry!). Most things we know and take for granted were unknown. Most of the questions hadn't even been thought of. No one looked for scientific, rational, provable answers to things. People's brains simply did not work in that way. What we now brush aside as whimsical and fanciful was for our ancient ancestors as normal and as valid as electricity is to us now. There was very little in the way of writing. Hardly anyone could read or write. There were no media. People simply didn't know what was happening beyond their own neighbourhood. Many didn't even know what, if anything, existed much beyond their own neighbourhood.

The worldview of our ancestors was shaped not by hard and fast scientifically provable fact, but rather by stories passed from one person to the next, from one community to the next, from one generation to the next. What we disparagingly dismiss as mystery, myth and legend were the very stuff of life for the ancients. They embraced the great mysteries that we abandon if we can't unpick them and prove them, and they weaved stories and word-pictures around them so that they could begin to grasp them and let them impact and shape their lives. The most obvious way of trying to make some sense out of a mystery is to anthropomorphise it, and so God became a man in the mind of humans.

That notion seems to have stuck in the human brain. It has survived the ages of enlightenment, industrial revolution, scientific discovery and digital revolution. Today's children, despite being hot-wired into this brave new world, have somehow inherited the notion of God as human being, a man who hears us and reacts to us, who makes stuff happen, who is in over-all control; and as they grow up they often, and unsurprisingly, find such a God to be a disappointment and a let-down.

When we begin to apply our reason, our enlightened thinking and our life experiences, we are surely bound to question whether the traditional understanding of God is sustainable in the world of today. Can we any longer simply and unquestioningly accept the received notions of an all loving God, a merciful God, a God who hears and answers our prayers, a God of "ask and you will receive", a God of peace? Is such an understanding of God really conscionable in the 21st century? Perhaps we should ask the innocent victims of war, torture, illness and bereavement. Surely we are bound to ask, 'Has he *really* made humankind in his own image?' If he has, some would argue that there's no wonder a lot of people don't rate him much. As we think of what is going on in the world, and maybe in our own lives, God seems either to be coldly, callously and cruelly in control or to be completely out of control. So where does that leave him? Can we really any longer claim him as the sentient, benevolent and omnipotent deity?

Sitting in front of the telly one Sunday evening, relaxing after the busyness of the day, and not long into a new post as vicar of some small villages in Somerset, the telephone rang.

The call shook me to the core and was just one more (albeit very major) experience causing me to question and re-think everything I had at one time simply accepted unquestioningly about God in general and the Christian faith in particular.

Not long before my arrival in the parish the much-loved and very talented teenaged organist at the church had died as a result of a brain tumour. He was one of two children in the family. His parents were crushed and their lives were turned upside-down. Now it was just the three of them: mum, dad and their elder son, Sam.[7]

The caller that Sunday evening had rung to tell me that that very evening Sam had been killed on his motorbike less than a mile from home.

What I had thought up until then was the solid rock of faith on which I stood, was shaken and began to slip away like dry sand in the wind.

The reading for the next Sunday happened to be from St John's Gospel where Mary's brother, Lazarus, is ill and Jesus is called, but he delays and arrives too late and Lazarus has already died. You can almost hear the bitterness, maybe even anger, in poor Mary's voice as she confronts Jesus – this so-called loving Son of a so-called loving God: 'Lord, if you had been here, my brother would not have died.'[8] To speak of a loving God to Sam's parents and to that village congregation could very understandably elicit a similar response: 'God, if you had been there, Sam would not have died. So where were you? Where are you? What kind of a God are you who would let this happen? Are you there at all?'

We read that 'God is love'.[9] Let's recall for a moment the tragic death of Sam in that motorbike accident. What are we to make of God in the light of such a horror? Maybe God simply is not in control, or maybe he's lost control, or, most worryingly of all, perhaps he exercises his control in a cold, callous and unloving way, picking and choosing his causes in a manner that seems so arbitrary and often so wrong. What kind of God is that? Such a God is wholly irreconcilable with a God who is love.

A God who consciously chooses to make everything happen, who omits to make or stop things happening, and who picks and chooses whose lot in life is going to be great and whose is going to be appalling, is not the kind of God I, along with many of us, want to have anything to do with. How can a God of love be reconciled with the bad stuff?

Maybe the truth of the situation is that God is not in control. He could be if he chose to be, but he chooses not to be. Maybe, contrary to what we traditionally believe, God is a "hands off" God rather than a "hands on" God. Maybe he leaves the world and the people in it to get on with it. It seems like that probably is the case, because if a loving God exercised control, if he was "hands on", there would surely be no earthquakes and tsunamis, there would be no wars and famines, there would be no illness and ghastly motor accidents.

But a God exercising control of his creation and letting earthquakes and tsunamis, wars and famines, illness and ghastly accidents happen would not be a loving God, but rather a horrid, cold, calculating, vindictive and cruel God, exercising control in the same way that totalitarian dictators exercise their control. Surely we couldn't invest in a God like that.

So it seems that if our God is a loving God, he's also a "hands off" God, not controlling anything much, if at all. It seems like that must be the case. And what's the good of that? Why is God like that? Why doesn't he get a grip?

Bad stuff happens and God is not to be hated or blamed for it. God is "hands off" not despite his love for us, but because of his love for us. He has set his creation and everything in it free from his controlling hand so that our lives, thoughts, experiences and emotions are real rather than merely the whim of the one pulling the strings; so that his love for us is real, so that our love for him is real, so that our love for one another is real and not merely a controlled contrivance.

Good and loving parents nurture their children, but the time comes when they let their children go free from their clutches and control. They let their children go out into the world to make of their lives what they will. They don't interfere, they don't insist that their off-spring lead the lives, make the relationships, go to the places and take the jobs they, the parents, want. No, they let their children go. They become "hands off" parents; they relinquish control. But do they stop loving their children, do they stop being interested in them, do they stop caring and worrying about them? Of course not! Parents probably love and care and worry about their precious children all the more because they have given up control and let them go.

It is right that parents should let them go. What kind of life would children have if they were completely controlled by mum and dad? 'Do as I say, go where I say, marry who I say, live where I say, take the job I dictate, bring your own children up my way.' That is not the truly loving way to deal with our children. The truly loving way is to let them be them: to release them completely into the world making sure they know in their hearts that their dad and mum will always love them, always care about them, always be there for them; nothing they might do could break the parent-child bond; they can always come to their folk who will be there with open arms for them –

not controlling, but quite simply loving. Is this not the picture of God's loving parenthood painted by Jesus in the story of The Prodigal Son?[10]

This is the only way a loving God can be reconciled with the kind of world we live in, with the kind of things that happen in it. God does not control. His creation - the world and everything in it, indeed the whole of creation - is free from his control *because* he loves what he has created. And like the great parent, he is always there, always loving, always caring, always worrying, always open-armed, always ready to welcome us if we go to him, but never controlling. So when tragedy strikes, God feels the pain. He weeps as Jesus wept at the death of his beloved friend Lazarus.[11]

Horror and tragedy are sometimes the way of an uncontrolled world, and God weeps for those touched by them. He knows the pain. He knows the suffering. He feels it just as keenly as Jesus felt those nails pierce his flesh. It hurts! God knows, it hurts! But we cling on to God like a hurt child clings to a parent, not because the parent can magically make the horror go away, but quite simply because the parent loves the child. We cling on to God because nothing, not even the most outrageous and horrific tragedy can separate us from his love.

I am convinced that neither death, nor life, nor angels, nor rulers, nor things present, nor things to come, nor powers, nor height, nor depth, nor anything else in all creation, will be able to separate us from the love of God in Christ Jesus our Lord. [12]

So What about Prayer?

If God is hands off, where does that leave intercessory prayer (prayerful petitioning)? What's the point of praying to God asking him to intervene in difficult situations? We do it all the time in church, and we are encouraged to lead prayerful lives outside church. We pray for people and situations – for change, for peace, for healing. What's the point if God is hands off? After all, if we are honest we must surely admit that although on rare occasions miracles do happen, in fact most of the time it feels like prayers are unanswered. The wars continue and the terminally sick die.

God is creation's author. He is Spirit. He is the Spirit of Love. He is not some puppet master pulling strings according to our direction. If he were, that would in fact make him the puppet and humans the grand puppet master. That would make us God.

Perhaps we expect too much, or the wrong thing, from intercessory prayer. To expect (or even demand) a miraculous, or a practical and mechanical answer to our prayers may be coming at prayer in the wrong way. Maybe intercessory prayer is not so much about how God can change a situation but rather how he can change us.

As the prodigal son returns into his father's presence and experiences his fathers compassion and love, the wayward lad is soothed, his mind and heart are set at peace and he experiences newness of life: '…this son of mine was dead and is alive again…'[13] As we spiritually put ourselves in God's presence through prayer and contemplation, we too will know his love and his peace which passes all understanding. We will know these things right there in the midst of whatever joy or sorrow we have in our hearts, and so we will be strengthened to go on, to keep going knowing that God always goes with us, that he loves us, but that he does not control us or manipulate our lives. That control is ours; it is the privilege, and sometimes the burden, of being free and really loved.

But can our prayers change things for those for whom we pray? A distressed adult pours out her heart to her loving mother. Her mother listens with care, compassion, patience

28

and love. Mother will probably not be able to do anything practical, but the very fact of being listened to and cared about soothes the child and may help her to see what she can do to change her own situation. The fact is that all too often we ourselves are the answer, or at least part of the answer, to our own prayers. The power to take some practical steps, to help, to comfort and console, and to bring about change, is ours and is often released in us as we bring our concerns to God. In this way those we pray for can be blessed.

There are, of course, those situations we pray about where we are powerless to do anything. We cannot bring an end to wars or prevent the suffering of refugees, and we can't miraculously heal sick bodies. We can cry out to God in sadness, desperation and even anger. The Psalms are full of sad, desperate and angry cries to God.

Awake, O Lord! Why do you sleep?
Arise! Do not reject us forever.
Why do you hide your face,
and forget our oppression and misery?
For our soul is brought low to the dust;
our body lies prostrate on the earth.
Stand up and come to our help!
Redeem us with your merciful love! [14]

Such prayers get it off our chest. God hears. He cares. He loves us and those we pray for. We will probably never know that as we pray, others somewhere else who *do* have the ability to do something might be being moved, prompted and equipped to act.

God is good, all good. Nothing that is bad is of God. But we know that there is bad stuff, and plenty of it. It is not from God; he is not responsible for it. And that is the struggle that is one of the great *realities and verities of existence*.

Chapter Three

The Bliss of Growth

Have You Seen the Glory?

"In the beginning when God created the heavens and the earth..." [15]

The world, indeed all of creation, really is extraordinary. Step aside from the daily round of busyness and put to one side the worries of your own life and the traumas of the world. It really is worth a look – a slow, deliberate, mindful look. For each of us different things will appeal. It might be looking out on a vast expanse of ocean with the fiery sun beginning to dip below the horizon. Perhaps it is the crisp, clear air of a snow-capped alpine beauty spot. Maybe the wonder is to be found in the intricate, wildly colourful and perfectly formed petals of our favourite spring flower. It could be the fascination of the grace and beauty of wildlife. Some folk love weather: sun, clouds, storms, wind and snow. Perhaps a teaming city filled with relentless energy and activity gives us a buzz, or it might be the sleepy charm of a quiet village, or the soul-feeding solitude of an empty, remote place. For me it is the sea.

I am writing these words as I sit at a cafe table overlooking the beach on a winter's day on the south coast of Brittany. The sun is bright and warming and the breeze is fresh. Folk are enjoying rippling conversation over good coffee and cigarettes. On the golden sand right in front of me a child, perhaps four or five, is kicking a football with his attentive dad. The view out to infinity (next stop Santander!) is beautiful. The sea is breaking gently and relentlessly on the shore. The scene is full of life and movement. There is a palpable sense of contentment and peace in the air. The atmosphere of benevolence, of love, is visceral, almost tangible. There must *surely* be something, perhaps someone, higher than ourselves, beyond ourselves, beyond our understanding holding this place, these people and this moment in time. Have you seen the glory?

Of course, it is not only in the natural world that life-giving beauty is to be found. Humans are capable of the most sublime creations. The soaring beauty of the great cathedrals, the choir within singing the evensong Psalms transporting us to the heavenlies; or for some it may be the thumping raw energy of hard rock or heavy metal. Art galleries are very popular. Queues can often be seen at the entrances to the great galleries in London, Rome, Florence and countless other places. People go because the pictures touch some inner part of their beings which yearn to be fed with beauty and with goodness. We are spiritual beings and we gravitate towards that which triggers our wonder and our awe. Have you seen the glory?

Creation, though, is not all breath-taking beauty and loveliness. It most certainly is not. Creation can wreak utter havoc, terror, misery and destruction, randomly and indiscriminately. I write this not long after central Italy has suffered one devastating and deadly earthquake after another over a six month period, causing death and terror: ancient mediaeval Tuscan towns and villages razed to the ground, homes and businesses lost, loved ones gone. At the same time in Syria the nightmare rages on as hate-filled human beings inflict hellish trauma and misery upon the innocent.

As I gaze upon tens of thousands of graves during my visits to the fields of Flanders at Remembrance time, I am reminded so powerfully of human kind's all too ready capacity to create hell on earth.

And yet there is something in the human spirit that never gives up. Places devastated by natural disaster are rebuilt. Communities start again, often better and stronger. Following the ravages of war, communities and countries usually pick themselves up and, with determination and renewed pride, strive to build a better future. The symbol of Remembrance Day is the red poppy which, every year since 1918, millions have pinned to their lapels in the early days of November. As that terrible war came to an end something remarkable happened. Out of the corpse-ridden, churned up, barbed wire-strewn countryside of Flanders, red poppies began to break the surface – splashes of colour breaking through the greyness, hints of new life in the fields of death, glimmers of hope, the tiniest hints of the glory of creation even in the pit of hell. Have you seen the glory?

Somewhere, somehow, often very easily missed, the glory is there. It might be some beautiful little natural reminder of life, like the poppy. More often, though, it is to be glimpsed in the presence, words and actions of other people. The day is grey, the money has run out, the body aches with flu and the cat has flees. Then the assistant at the checkout smiles, packs your shopping for you, touches your hand as she gives you change and says a kind word as you leave. As you stagger with your shopping towards your front door, the locally-feared, shaven-headed, pierced and tattooed mischief-maker offers to carry your bags to the door for you and maybe your neighbour, noticing that you're under the weather, brings round a steaming casserole for the family's supper. Or maybe it's simpler and less obvious: your colleague at work smiles at you just when you could do with seeing a smile; something you're working on seems to be going okay when you fully expected it to go badly wrong; the doctor has more time and attention for you than you anticipated - glimmers, hints, tastes of the glory.

The Author of Life

This is the great mystery: what happened "in the beginning"? For people of Abrahamic tradition – Jews, Moslems and Christians – the traditional answer is to be found in the first book of the Hebrew Bible - The Old Testament. Genesis chapter one gives us the well-known account of the six-day creation with God as the master creator. Many of us now believe that the way in which the world was actually created was very different indeed. We have been enlightened by science. In the second chapter of Genesis we read of how

God created humankind in the well-known Adam and Eve story. Again, many of us now believe that the way humans actually came into being was very different. We have been enlightened by evolutionary discovery. The remainder of the Old Testament is about the highs and lows of the story of humankind from the very start, culminating in a much-needed redemptive and saving intervention by God to put right the utter mess humans had made of God's perfect creation. The stories are extraordinary, exciting, confusing and at time downright horrific and even offensive.

God tested Abraham. He said to him, 'Abraham!' And he said, 'Here I am.' He said, 'Take your son, your only son Isaac, whom you love, and go to the land of Moriah, and offer him there as a burnt-offering on one of the mountains that I shall show you.' [16]

What kind of a God would ask such a thing?

But as for the towns of these peoples that the Lord your God is giving you as an inheritance, you must not let anything that breathes remain alive. You shall annihilate them—the Hittites and the

36

Amorites, the Canaanites and the Perizzites, the
Hivites and the Jebusites—just as the Lord your
God has commanded…[17]

Does God demand genocide?

The Next day an evil spirit from God rushed upon Saul.[18]

If God is all-good and all-loving, and fully in control, and if the works of the devil (evil) are his enemy, what on earth is he doing imposing evil spirits upon people?

These are just the tiniest examples of the numerous accounts in the Old Testament of God-commanded and God-inspired violence, destruction and extermination. The historical basis of many of these stories is very questionable, and of course it must be remembered that the written accounts which we now call "Holy Writ" were written down a very long time indeed after the purported events.

The Middle Eastern community of three and a half thousand years ago gathered around an unfolding story in its search for answers. The story was handed down largely by word of mouth by people without any knowledge of science. The story was very loosely based on a vague notion of some of the events that had happened in times passed, and always augmented by imaginings, myths and supernatural tales. This was not regarded as fantasy or fiction in the minds of folk who had absolutely no concept of scientific explanation. Story, myth and imagination were wholly normal ways of understanding the world, of describing and understanding God, of conveying "fact".

This was a nomadic society. There were lots of tribes and little kingdoms constantly at war with one another. There were suffering and slaughter. There was a constant battle against the elements. The stories were set in that context, in the worldview of those people in that place and time. The stories often seem odd to us now; they seem violent and totally at odds with the way we see things. Hardly surprising! We live in the twenty-first century western world. Our understanding of the world, our mindset, our culture and our experience are a million miles away from that of the Old Testament world. So who *is* this God who set it all in motion?

Scientists think the earth is about 4.5 billion years old and that the universe was created over 13 billion years ago. We are inclined to think that creation was something that happened a long time ago, that somehow creation is done and dusted and that we are living in the finished product. The reality is different.

Creation is a continuing event. It might have begun all those billions of years ago, but it is certainly not finished; it is continuing. We are living in the midst of creation. It continues to happen all around us. The continual shifting, shaking and exploding of our world is evidence enough of that. Astronomers looking deep into space are able to see stars being born and stars dying. The universe is a bubbling cauldron of movement and change. Scientists say it is expanding all the time. Things will look very, very different indeed in another billion years. Our world and the universe will be unrecognisable; and Homo Sapiens will almost certainly have disappeared, having been, for a brief time, just another of nature's creatures along the way.

The continuing business of creation is an awesome and wonderful thing. Our world is extraordinarily created – just right for the flourishing of the animal and plant life of which we humans are a part. The world is burgeoning with growth. Everything grows the whole time. We know that well enough when we leave our garden unattended for too long. Animal life constantly grows – from conception to birth to adulthood to death. There's constant change. Nothing stays the same even for a moment.

That is creation. It is wonderful, amazing, and endlessly fascinating. Scientists can explain things in so much detail, but the explanations can only ever go so far. Ultimately there is what will forever remain an unknown that is the author of creation. The word, the name, that many people give to this source is "God". And if creation is a continuing business then that mystery which is behind it, which is driving it – God, is continuing, ever present and ever active. God is present and ever active in creation as it rolls on out there and around us. It follows, therefore, that God is present and ever active with respect to us too, because each one of us is a part of that continual creativity. The biological, chemical and electrical processes that make us what we are, continue relentlessly to keep going every second that goes by. It is called "life". It is not only a matter of the physical stuff, though. We are conscious, thinking beings. Our thought processes, our feelings and our emotions, both good and bad, are all part and parcel of continuing creation, and so God is present and active in them too. We are thinking, spiritual beings who wonder at the mysteries of creation, life and death.

As far back as history can take us there is clear evidence of human spirituality. What urged our ancestors of four or five thousand years ago to quarry and then drag vast multi-tonne stones over many miles to construct Stonehenge? And there is archaeological evidence of similar constructions going as far back as 8,000 B.C. That these structures played an important part in ritual and worship is in little doubt. There is something in the heart of human beings which points us towards a higher power outside of ourselves. It is irresistible – hard-wired into our minds and souls, and the urge is to worship that higher power in awe and reverence, and to invoke and petition "him" for our welfare and wellbeing. We are indeed spiritual beings, and so it makes absolute sense to claim that we are made in God's image if we understand God not as some kind of invisible, heavenly man, but as spirit. The Bible is clear on spirit as being the nature and identity of God. John's Gospel reports Jesus telling the woman at the well: 'God is spirit, and those who worship him must worship in spirit and truth.'[19] God is Spirit, not flesh, and we humans are made in his image.

We have already considered the horrors of the world and of human experience. They are part and parcel of the constant creative activity which is existence. So, is God, the creating author, the creator of the bad stuff as well as the good stuff?

There is something in the human mind that distinguishes good from bad. Most of us gravitate towards and yearn for all that is good, and we despise what is bad and hateful. We tend to rail at God for allowing the bad stuff to happen. But if we are made in the image of God, then that gravitation towards good, that yearning for good, that despising of all that is bad and hateful, must be something we have inherited from God. They must be intrinsically God qualities.

Whilst many, perhaps most, Christian folk do not read the Genesis creation stories as historical fact, these stories remain of very great value in telling us about the nature of God and his dealings with humans.

The first chapter of Genesis endorses the notion that God is good. He is the creative Spirit who has made things "good".[20] Among the things "made good" by God are human beings whom he made in his image and whom he blessed.[21] We read, 'God saw everything that he had made, and indeed, it was very good.'[22] That includes us!

There is a largely accepted Christian doctrine which says that human beings are inherently sinful, that they are born sinners; it is called the doctrine of original sin. It is predicated on the idea that every human being is a direct descendant of the first humans, Adam and Eve, and that every human has inherited their sinfulness (disobeying God by eating the forbidden apple). The doctrine finds its roots in the 2nd century Bishop, Irenaeus. St Augustine developed the doctrine, and it was later embraced by protestant reformers and continues to be held today in many Christian circles.

Those of you who, like me, were present at the birth of your children may struggle, as I do, with the notion that these achingly beautiful and extraordinary creations arrive into the world sinful. The very idea is so totally at odds with a God who, we are told both in scripture and also by a reading of our own human instinct, creates good. God is the author and creator of good, not bad. Perhaps it is no coincidence that the words "God" and "good" are very similar.

Returning to Adam and Eve, perhaps this is a story not so much about how sin entered into the world; perhaps it is not the foundation for a doctrine of original sin; perhaps instead, it is about God loving human beings and wanting them to know that they are truly loved – a love that can only be given and received when control is relinquished. The apple tree incident was the gift of freedom from control which carries with it the possibility of knowing real love, but also the burden of choice-making and its consequences – the cross that we have to bear, the cross which is the price of freedom and love.

However, our God-given, lovingly given, freedom does bring out in us what we might call the *urge towards self*, or the *selfish gene*. If there is any sense in which humans are born sinful, then this is it: that we urge towards self. It is part of our animal instinct, for that is what we are - animals. We have an innate urge for self-preservation, for food, to procreate (and therefore for sex), for power, for territorial dominion and ultimately for survival for us and our off-spring. All of that comes from God because he created us to be free animals in a free world with the purpose that we should "go forth and multiply". Followers of Christ have those strong urges as much as anyone else. Not surprising then that history shows Christians to have taken the principle of goodness, of Godliness, which is at large in creation, and to have codified it, institutionalised it, dogmatised it and developed doctrine around it. In this way it becomes possible to discriminate between those who are in and those who are out. In this way rules are created which keep some in power and others in servitude. Primacy and superiority can be asserted.

Christian doctrine and dogma are not of God. They don't exist as definite, distinct, created things; rather they are the product of the human selfish gene asserting itself. They are the way in which, for many Christians, survival of the fittest is worked out. Jesus did not create doctrine and dogma. He lived a certain kind of life within a certain cultural and contextual background and understanding. Many of us choose, broadly, to follow in his way; and of course, we are completely free to pick and choose what of him we follow, or indeed not to follow him at all.

Power to the Faint and Strength to the Weary

Some years ago a good friend was preparing to take a three month sabbatical. He and his wife were going to join a party of trekkers making their way to just above base camp on Mount Everest. There was no doubt this was going to be an extremely challenging and often uncomfortable experience. Altitude, cold and sheer exhaustion from miles and miles of rough-terrain walking would surely take its toll. Many of those who attempt this adventure drop out along the way, but Rob and Sue were fit and enthusiastic. They were determined to finish. My wife, Karen, and I prayed for and with them as they prepared.

As they departed for their adventure, we gave Rob and Sue a little gift to take with them: a bar of Kendall Mint Cake only to be consumed in a moment of crippling exhaustion and flagging spirits, and alongside that a sealed envelope containing a card bearing a few words of encouragement to be opened and read during that difficult Kendal Mint Cake moment.

Some weeks later Rob and Sue returned from their expedition. They had made it! They had been part way up Mount Everest and had looked down upon Base Camp

(17,600ft)! What became, we wondered, of the little gift? Their story goes like this.

They were many days into the hike and were feeling the effects of the high altitude. The terrain was becoming more and more difficult – rough, narrow and precipitous. The weather was closing in. It was extremely cold – way, way below freezing – and the freezing mist was descending as the clouds rolled in around them. They were completely done in. Their bodies ached with strain and fatigue. Their spirits were at their lowest possible ebb. Maybe, there on that cloud covered freezing mountainside, it was time to give up. They had to rest; they parked their backsides on the rocks and sat there peering into the frozen pea-soup gloom. What to do?

Ah! Time to open the emergency gift! Rob and Sue rummaged in their backpacks and found the little parcel. They ripped it open and began to gorge, gratefully, on the Kendall Mint Cake. The minty freshness, combined with the mega-dose of sugar, revived them a little. Then they opened the envelope.

We had chosen a postcard of a sun-drenched mountain scene with an elegant golden eagle gliding gracefully and majestically across the valley. The picture bore some words from Isaiah:

He gives power to the faint,

and strengthens the powerless.

Even youths will faint and be weary,

and the young will fall exhausted;

but those who wait for the Lord shall renew

their strength,

they shall mount up with wings like eagles,

they shall run and not be weary,

they shall walk and not faint. [23]

At the very moment Rob and Sue looked at the card and read those words, something remarkable happened. The clouds around them began to disperse. The freezing drizzle stopped. The sun began to break through – warm, bright and life-giving; and as the splendour of the Himalayan ranges came into view, there, right in front of them, soaring across the valley, was a golden eagle. They marvelled at the wonder of the scene before them; it literally buzzed with God's creative presence. They were physically and spiritually refreshed and restored, ready to go on and conquer this beautiful mountain – well, half of it at any rate! They had seen the glory. They were blessed and touched by *the bliss of growth.*

Chapter Four

The Splendour of Action

My mum and dad were always big on table manners. Table manners are not an easy lesson to teach growing, wilful children! Chew with your mouth closed. Elbows off the table. Say "Please and thank you". Don't reach across the table. Ask for the food to be passed. Please, please don't swing on your chair! Let others fill their plates first.

What is that all about? Why are table manners, indeed why is the whole complicated code of etiquette and manners, important at all? In essence manners are all about putting others before self by being respectful of them and showing a humble, servant attitude.

Any aristocrats among you, and all of those who lapped up Downton Abbey on the television, or any of the other numerous period costume dramas, will know that in upper-class households the staff first feed the dinner guests in the dining room, and only after the dinner is served and finished do the servants go into the kitchen and eat. Servants always put others first.

We've seen that at the very core of an understanding of God is love. We read in scripture that "God is love, and those who abide in love abide in God, and God abides in them."[24] For a very great many people, an understanding of love, and therefore of God, becomes possible because of Jesus.

Jesus knew a lot about table manners and having a humble, servant attitude. Many of his reported encounters with people revolved around food and drink: the wedding at Cana,[25] the feeding of the five thousand,[26] the meal at Levi's house with sinners and tax collectors,[27] the rather awkward meal at the Pharisee's house,[28] and another meal at a Pharisee's house when Jesus told the assembled company stories about meals![29] And, of course, the meal in the upper room was all about serving others, putting others first, humbling oneself and making sacrifices so that others might benefit: 'This is my body I am giving for you; this is my blood which is poured out for you.' It is a meal, *this* meal, which is at the heart of Christian worship and ritual.[30] This is not an exhaustive list of the meals we read of Jesus sharing, and no doubt there were probably hundreds more that have gone unreported. It could be said that Jesus ate his way through the Gospels!

Jesus used meals as occasions to build relationships and form bonds with others, often the most unlikely others, and as opportunities to demonstrate and explain true servantheartedness and true love. His shared meals and food-based parables were lessons in good manners, that is to say in respect and in love: make sure the wedding guests do not go thirsty;[31] honour your loved ones by serving the best food;[32] don't pick the best seat at the table for yourself;[33] don't always just invite your friends to dinner, but invite the struggling stranger, the unloved and the unlovely;[34] get up and feed those midnight visitors;[35] don't send your guest home hungry because they might faint on the way.[36]

Jesus used the dinner table to teach all sorts of lessons, but above all to show and explain love.

For those who go to the Bible for the final word on any topic, it is unequivocal about God, about who he is. The Bible is very clear: "God is love".[37] We have established that the source and sustainer of continuing creation is God, but that there are many horrors of growth as well as the bliss of growth. So what are we to make of the notion that God is love?

There is something deep within the human psyche that knows about and gravitates towards love. We all want good relationships with others, we all want peace, and we all shudder at the ghastliness which too many people in the world suffer. Even those who mete out suffering have the capacity to care and love, however deeply hidden and repressed it may be.

Care, compassion and love are natural human instincts; they are God-created. Parents know that to be true. We quite simply love our children come what may. We may not always approve of what they do or say, we may not always like them, the relationship may even have broken down, but we cannot stop loving them; they are our children, after all.

What do we mean by the word "love"? Our language is very lacking in this regard. We have only the one word, "love", to cover a multitude of meanings. We love our children and we love chocolate. Hardly the same thing! When we talk of "making love" we are usually referring to the act of sexual intercourse. Such an act may or may not take place between people who actually love one another, and, of course, there are plenty of couples who deeply love one another who, for whatever reason, don't "make love". Furthermore, when we speak of loving our siblings and our friends, we are usually talking about rather a different kind of love from the love we have for our spouse or partner. All of the kinds of love just mentioned are to do with feelings, emotions and physical gratification. Greek, the language of the New Testament, is much better than English at talking about them.

New Testament Greek has four entirely different words for love, each referring to a different kind of love. If we were to read the New Testament in its original Greek, we would be surprised to see that wherever we read "love" in English translations, the Greek text uses different words (one of the four) in order to make clear what kind of love is being talked about. How much easier it would be if we had a similar system in English. There would be much less scope for misunderstanding.

Let's look at the four kinds of love to be found in New Testament Greek.

Éros (ἔρως) is used to speak of physical attraction and of passionate, intimate love which probably involves (or aspires to) sexual activity.

Philia (φιλία) refers to that affectionate regard and loyalty experienced between good friends and relations.

Storge (στοργή) is all about a very special bond of care and affection – the kind that usually exists between parents and children, involving a deep, natural empathy and concern.

Agápe (ἀγάπη) is unconditional love - a regard, concern, compassion for and a willingness to help another person without any thought of fairness, any expectation of reciprocation, or any consideration of deserving. It involves the absolute abandonment of self in favour of a pure desire for the good of the other person.

This last kind of love, *agape* love, might involve emotions and feelings, but not necessarily. It is sometimes said that this kind of love is more a verb than a noun. With *agape*, we *do* love rather than necessarily feel it.

Let's look at what kinds of love are being spoken of in key New Testament passages on the subject by checking out which Greek word the text uses.

We'll look first at that definitive statement about God in John's first letter: "God is love".[38] Here the original Greek text uses the word *agape*. In St John's Gospel, when Jesus is having his final instructive discourse with his friends on the night before he died, he tells them:

> *"I give you a new commandment, that you love one another. Just as I have loved you, you also should love one another. By this everyone will know that you are my disciples, if you have love for one another."*[39]

In each instance of the word "love", *agape* is used. Then there is what is sometimes called *The Golden Rule* or *The Greatest Commandment*. Jesus said that everything hangs on this rule or commandment. It is found in three of the four Gospels. Here it is from St Matthew:

'"You shall love the Lord your God with all your heart, and with all your soul, and with all your mind." This is the greatest and first commandment. And a second is like it: "You shall love your neighbour as yourself." On these two commandments hang all the law and the prophets.'[40]

Every time the word "love" appears in this passage, and in the similar passages in the other Gospels, [16] the Greek text uses the word *agape*.

It is abundantly clear that Jesus was encouraging his followers to *do* love, to show care, compassion and concern for others and to help them in practical ways all for the good of the other, and all entirely unconditionally, without thought of reciprocation and whether or not they considered the other person to be deserving. This kind of love is pragmatic. It is often sacrificial. It involves an abandonment of self - a setting aside of prejudices, likes and dislikes, considerations of convenience, concerns about hardship to self, political and religious and cultural preferences and opinions – all of these things are disregarded; they have no place in *agape* love.

Agape love is tough; it is completely counter-cultural; it may well go against all our instincts. Jesus explained something of what it might involve:

'Love[41] your enemies, do good to those who hate you, bless those who curse you, pray for those who abuse you. If anyone strikes you on the cheek, offer the other also; and from anyone who takes away your coat do not withhold even your shirt. Give to everyone who begs from you; and if anyone takes away your goods, do not ask for them again.' [42]

The Gospels are littered with examples of Jesus showing *agape* love to others in words and deeds. The love he demonstrated was often counter-cultural, that is to say it involved words and behaviour that were contrary to many of the social, religious and political norms of the day; and indeed many of his demonstrations of love were regarded as blasphemous and deeply offensive breaches of religious laws, and therefore deserving of punishment.

In the time and place of Jesus' ministry, the physically and mentally sick and disabled were rejected from society. Some ailments in particular were singled out as being wholly unacceptable. The mentally afflicted were regarded as demon-possessed and were left entirely to fend for themselves outside communities, families and fellowships.

In Mark's Gospel we read about Jesus' encounter with the Gerasene demoniac, a man possessed by "unclean spirits", who "lived among the tombs" and "on the mountains".[43] We have no idea what was actually wrong with him. It is probable that he was in fact suffering from some kind of paranoid schizophrenia which today is recognised as a diagnosable and treatable illness. For a first century Middle Eastern community the attitude was "out of sight, out of mind", and if the poor sufferer just wouldn't stay away, then he needed to be restrained and shackled with chains.[44] The social norm was to reject or restrain. Jesus, however, broke all the social norms, fears and taboos, and approached the man and healed him. This demonstration of *agape* love had consequences for Jesus: the bystanders were afraid, they reported Jesus to the authorities and he was told to leave.[45] Jesus' love for the sufferer was selfless and sacrificial.

Another ailment to be singled out as being wholly unacceptable was menstrual bleeding. Of course today, thank goodness, it is not regarded as an ailment at all, but simply as a natural part of nature's reproductive process - a part, if you like, of the *bliss of growth*. But for the folk of Jesus' time it was a disgusting, unclean taboo. This is the ancient Jewish law on the matter:

When a woman has a discharge of blood that is her regular discharge from her body, she shall be in her impurity for seven days, and whoever touches her shall be unclean until the evening. Everything upon which she lies during her impurity shall be unclean; everything also upon which she sits shall be unclean. Whoever touches her bed shall wash his clothes, and bathe in water, and be unclean until the evening. Whoever touches anything upon which she sits shall wash his clothes, and bathe in water, and be unclean until the evening; whether it is the bed or anything upon which she sits, when he touches it he shall be unclean until the evening. If any man lies with her, and her impurity falls on him, he shall be unclean for seven days; and every bed on which he lies shall be unclean.

If a woman has a discharge of blood for many days, not at the time of her impurity, or if she has a discharge beyond the time of her impurity, for all the days of the discharge she shall continue in uncleanness; as in the days of her impurity, she shall be unclean.[46]

So, imagine the kind of life that a poor woman who had been bleeding for twelve years would have. It is just such a woman whom Jesus encounters not long after the demoniac episode.[47] Imagine her plight. She would have been in constant pain; she would have been exhausted and weak from the constant loss of blood. But her condition not only carried with it physical difficulties; what a spiritual and cultural burden this must also have been. She carried a stigma, a terrible stigma. She would have been labelled "unclean". People would have gone out of their way to avoid her, and she would have gone out of her way to avoid coming into contact with others. Her life would have been one of lonely isolation with no prospect of forming any meaningful relationships, let alone enjoying a married life. Not only would others have thought of her as "unclean", but she too would have considered herself to be "unclean" – permanently unclean. She would have been shunned, avoided, lonely, isolated, dirty, worthless and good for nothing. It was not her own fault, but nevertheless that was her lot in life. What an immense and unbearable burden to carry. She would probably have been angry, bitter, sad and resentful.

The Jewish law was very clear on the matter: she's unclean; keep away! But instead Jesus is not in the least phased when she touches his cloak. He doesn't ignore her, he doesn't berate her; he doesn't shoo her away and he doesn't try to run away from her. That is how the religious leaders would have reacted. That's probably how almost anybody would have reacted, but not Jesus. As the woman in healed, Jesus quite simply loves her with the words, 'Daughter, your faith has made you well; go in peace, and be healed of your disease.'[48]

The woman's healing was physical; her bleeding stopped. Certainly that was wonderful. But imagine how her life was transformed in so many other ways too: no longer "unclean", no longer an outcast, no longer shunned and avoided at every twist and turn, no longer isolated, no longer having to be lonely, the opportunity to engage with people at last, the opportunity to form loving and close relationships, and maybe even the opportunity for marriage and children. At last she had a chance for life in all its fullness. Jesus said to her, 'Go in peace.' The real healing was the peace, her peace with the world and her own deep inner peace which Jesus gave her as he took her brokenness, her burden, from her. He broke the law to do that. He offended the religious leaders and others besides. He was taking a personal risk, but his heart and mind were always focussed on the woman, on loving her.

There are numerous other examples in the Gospels of Jesus' miraculous healings which are all demonstrations of transformational love, *agape* love.

Jesus demonstrated such a love in other ways too. He abandoned his own safety, and any thought of having a good reputation, by demonstrating Godly love to the people others loved to hate, to people considered sinful and unworthy of God's love.

Adultery was a sin against God's holy law as given to Moses in the Ten Commandments: "You shall not commit adultery."[49] The penalty laid down for those caught in adultery was death.

If a man commits adultery with the wife of his neighbour, both the adulterer and the adulteress shall be put to death.[50]

If a man is caught lying with the wife of another man, both of them shall die, the man who lay with the woman as well as the woman.[51]

Anyone caught in the act would usually be stoned to death. So when the religious leaders brought a guilty woman to Jesus, all ready to stone her to death, they put Jesus' radical, illegal and counter-cultural love to the test. 'The Law says we should stone her to death; what do you say?' He caught them out with his suggestion that if any of them were sinless they should cast the first stone. They knew that they, like all of us, get things wrong from time to time, and so chastened, they drifted away, defeated. As for the guilty woman, Jesus did not condemn. It is tragic when Christians judge and condemn others. Jesus was not into judging and condemning; he was into loving. He reserved his condemnation and contempt for the self-satisfied religious folk who loved to condemn and judge. Instead, Jesus blessed the woman with extraordinary love, with God's love. He said, 'Neither do I condemn you. Go on your way, and from now on do not sin again.'[52]

The woman was given a clean slate and a fresh start. This is what Jesus did. He gave people the chance of fresh starts over and over again. This is what God does; he gives us the chance of fresh starts over and over again.

Going back to meals for a moment, it was a customary mark of welcome and respect in that place and time for a host to kiss his guests and to provide water for them to wash their feet. On one occasion when Jesus was eating at the house of a religious leader, a woman of ill repute (we can guess she was probably a prostitute) burst in carrying a jar of very, very expensive ointment. She started wiping Jesus' feet with the precious stuff, bathing his feet with her tears and wiping them dry with her hair. What a display of emotion and devotion! Jesus' host was tutting away thinking, 'if only Jesus knew what kind of a woman this was, he'd send her away with a flea in her ear.' Instead Jesus rebuked his host and reminded him that he hadn't even welcomed Jesus with a kiss, let alone provide some water for foot washing. Jesus lovingly allowed the woman to continue with her devotions and he concluded by telling her that her sins were forgiven and that she could go in peace. There it is again – Jesus offering the chance of a fresh start! The other important guests were startled, affronted and offended.[53] Jesus really did love without having any regard for the consequences to himself.

The ultimate demonstration of love, of agape love, shown by Jesus was at his crucifixion. He had been brutally arrested, tormented, ridiculed and humiliated. He was flogged almost to the point of death and then ordered to carry his own cross through the narrow streets and up a steep and rough pathway to the top of a hill. There he was stripped naked and long nails were driven through his wrists and ankles into the rough and splintered wood of a cross. The cross was roughly hauled up and dropped heavily into a hole in the ground. The pain cannot be adequately imagined. Then he was left in the heat of the midday Mediterranean sun to die. As he hanged there waiting for death to overcome him, he looked upon the soldiers who had just nailed him to the cross and he uttered these words:

'Father, forgive them; for they do not know what they are doing.' [54]

Even at the point of a murderous and unjust death, Jesus was still loving – still loving those whom others might regard as undeserving, still loving without regard for himself, still demonstrating Godly love. And, of course, the great assurance for us in this scene is that if God can forgive Jesus' executioners, then he can surely forgive every one of us too. It is interesting to note that the soldiers did not ask for forgiveness, but Jesus gave it anyway. That is truly radical, and some may say offensive, love.

Again, there are numerous other examples in the Gospels of Jesus' counter-cultural and non-judgmental refusal to condemn which are all demonstrations of transformational love, *agape* love.

It doesn't really matter what we think about the possibility of miraculous healings and whether they can really happen. The point of the healing stories is not about that. The point of all these stories is to show us what love – selfless, unconditional, *agape* love – is like, to show us what God's love for us is like, and to give us an example to follow. We are not being asked to perform miraculous healings, but we are being encouraged to love (*agape*) our neighbour, to love the people we encounter on a day to day basis as we go about our lives. And why should we love like that? So that we might be agents of God's love; so that there may be change and transformation – change from the worries and burdens, trials and difficulties, sadnesses and self-doubt that everyone experiences at one time or another; so that those we love, and we ourselves, might truly live and "go in peace". Jesus is our example and Christians are called to follow him. Imagine what the world would be like if every human being loved (*agape*) in that way! Maybe that is what it means when we pray for God's Kingdom to come on earth as it is heaven.

In the early days of Christianity Christians were not called "Christians". Christianity as a separate "religion" did not exist as such. Jesus and his followers were Jews. It is worth remembering that Jesus was brought up and tutored in the Jewish faith. He was steeped in the Jewish scriptures. He didn't regard himself as the inventor of a new religion. Many viewed him and his followers as some kind of Jewish sect. His purpose was to demonstrate the love of God and to show people how to love (*agape*) so that life could be different, better, experienced as best as it could possibly be; so that life could be lived in all its fullness.

The early followers were not called "Christians", they were called "Followers of The Way"[55] – the way of Jesus. Jesus called those around him to 'Take up your cross and follow me'.[56] As Christians today, the calling is upon us to take up our crosses – our frailties, fears and inadequacies – and to follow Jesus, to follow his way as the pattern for our own lives. The commitment we make and the standard to which we aspire, is to obey Jesus' *Golden Rule*[57] that we love (*agape*) our neighbours, that is, the people we encounter in the daily round of life. These days the word "Christian" is heavily loaded with all sorts of stereotypes, preconceptions and misconceptions. What comes to the mind of many non-Christians when they hear the word is probably church buildings, priests in strange clothing, irrelevant and boring services, hypocrites and self-righteous judgment makers. Maybe the time has come to restore and reclaim the moniker "Followers of The Way".

One of the great objections to Christianity in general and to Christians in particular is that they are hypocrites, that they talk so highly and piously of love, care and forgiveness and yet seem to fail in these qualities, and indeed to present all too often as exclusive, superior and judgmental. Sadly there seems to be an element of truth in such a charge. However, such

65

apparent failings on the part of Christians are not good reason for rejecting Christianity. Most, perhaps all, people who claim to be Christian at least *aspire* to the Way of Jesus. Any state of perfection can only ever be aspirational, and it must surely be laudable to have such an aspiration, although praise is not (or should not be) what Christians are after.

What about the cross? What was that all about? Christians draw from the crucifixion profound and multi-layered meaning. 'Somehow', we say, 'it is Jesus' sacrifice on the cross that saves us.' That is a lovely sentiment and idea, but how does it actually work? How does the brutal death of this man of love save us, and from what?

God is love, and Jesus is the perfect, living human example (incarnation) of the God who is love. We therefore speak of Jesus' deity, of his perfect Godliness. There are others in history that have been remarkable in living out *agape* love, who are driven by a desire for the well-being of others, by a desire for justice for others. We could name some: Mahatma Ghandi, Mother Teresa, Florence Nightingale, The Dalai Lama, Guru Nanak, Mirza Masroor Ahmad,[58] and there are very many others. It may be that we have our favourite whom we revere and whose life we hold as the pattern for our own, or at least aspire to. For Christians that one is Jesus, the God of active, *agape* love.

Jesus loved completely and with total commitment, even to the point of dying. When Jesus died on the cross he was being punished for nothing; he had done nothing wrong. The only thing he ever did was to love people actively, caringly, helpfully, inclusively and justly. He loved everyone, even those whom most others despised or didn't trust, or frowned upon. He loved them all. And he wouldn't stop loving even when the political and religious leaders got angry, even when they were jealous of his popularity. Jesus just kept right on loving and forgiving and caring and mending, until in the end his love killed him. The leaders couldn't take any more of him, so they executed him on a cross. And even then, he looked down at the soldiers who nailed him to it and prayed, 'Father forgive them,'[59] and he looked into the eyes of the robber who was hanging on a cross next to him and said to him, 'Today you will be with me in paradise.'[60] He loved so much and so well that he was killed for it. He quite literally "loved to death".

Jesus lived completely and fully in the stream of goodness and creativity that is God, and as Christians we seek to follow him. His dying for the sake of love must surely have a lasting and enduring effect. This lasting and enduring effect is the power of the cross which can only be completed by the resurrection. Those who follow Christ *are* the resurrected Christ, are the body of Christ, indeed are Christ in the world today. So yes, we can say that Jesus lives – in those who attempt to live in his generous example. He is gone, but his spirit, his philosophy, his love – his Godly love - live on through us today. And why do we follow him? For our own gain? To secure a place in heaven? Out of duty or fear? No; it is all for the sake of love – Godly, *agape* love which promotes unity, peace, joy, contentment, enough of what we need – the Kingdom of God.

Jesus *does* live on in our midst, and in that sense too he is resurrected. He does make himself known again and again. When we gather around the altar and receive the bread and the cup, is he not right there in our midst? When the word or touch or deed of another brightens our day, changes our mood, lifts our heart, is he not there then? When we stand awestruck in the face of a breathtaking view, a stunning work of art, a most utterly beautiful piece of music, is he not there then? When we know that people are praying for us, and that makes a difference to us in our hearts and gives us a sense of peace, is he not there then?

But we so often miss Jesus. In the busy bustle of life we miss his presence, we miss his touch, we miss those pearls of grace: the kind word, the gentle touch, the scent of flowers on the breeze, the rippling laughter of a child, the little event that happens at precisely the right time for us, the phrase in a book or paper or on a billboard that makes us laugh. Jesus is there then. He's with us day by day and moment by moment. Do we see? Are the eyes of our hearts open? Are they ready to catch sight of Jesus in the ordinariness of our daily lives?

And are we ready to *be* the eyes, the voice and the hands of Jesus? Are we ready to *be* the resurrected, living Christ? Are we ready to seize every opportunity to follow his pattern of love, to be the one giving a reassuring smile, saying a kind word, carrying someone's load for part of the way, being a shoulder to cry on, being a hugger always ready to hug someone back to life? Are we on the look out? Are we ready? We surely don't want ourselves and others to be carried away so completely by the hustle and hassle of life that we miss out on seeing the love and grace of Jesus at work in the world before our very eyes.

The work and power of the cross, together with the resurrection, is that through them we can be saved from the worst excesses of the *urge towards self* which, left to its own devices, can easily be unfulfilling and, at worst, lead to misery and wretchedness. Conversely, the splendour of the Godly *agape* love of Jesus to which Christian people aspire - *the splendour of action* - can change the world.

Chapter Five

The Glory of Power

I mentioned in an earlier chapter that during the writing of this I spent some time in Brittany. It was wonderful to visit the multitude of medieval cathedrals and churches in that part of France and to sit awhile in them.

Quimper cathedral is utterly beautiful. People don't just build such buildings for no reason, or simply to show off how well they can build, or to make a power statement. These places are the glory of the human creative spirit. They somehow "hold" the author of creation. The very air hums, as if electrically charged, with the presence of *creative bliss, splendid action* and *glorious power.* An energy of goodness and love flows around the columns and dances amongst the coloured shafts streaming from the windows. The space is both still and vibrant. The whole place tells a story which touches the heart, which quietens the mind and which nourishes the soul.

When we travel to new cities in this country or further afield, is it not often the local cathedral or the peaceful country church, or the windswept cemetery to which we turn? Cathedrals are busy places and many of them are great tourist attractions. On their journey through life people so often stop awhile at the nearest place of worship whether or not they confess to a religious faith, in order to find beauty, wonder, mystery and peace. These waymarks on our journey are reminders of the Other, the higher power beyond ourselves that we call God; and more often than not, having stopped awhile at these spiritual watering holes, the traveller moves on refreshed, inspired and more at peace with him or herself and more at peace with the world.

In chapter two we reminded ourselves that God is love.[61] We also read in the Bible that 'God is Spirit'.[62] It is not hard to accept this when surrounded by the beauty, tranquillity and peace of a magnificent cathedral or quiet country church. But God doesn't just live in churches. The God of creation lives in all of creation, and has always done so right from the very beginning of creation. Indeed the Spirit of God existed before all else. God's Spirit pre-existed existence.

> *In the beginning when God created the heavens and the earth, the earth was a formless void and darkness covered the face of the deep, while a wind from [or, the Spirit of] God swept over the face of the waters.*[63]

God is the unknown and unseeable mystery, the author of creation. Whether he is person, spirit, power, energy, whatever, he is the final answer, the ultimate truth which will always be unfathomable. He has created utter beauty, abundance and love, all of which, out of love, he has set free, and from which he has relinquished any kind of manipulating control. The result is that alongside the *bliss of creation* there is also horror, violence, destruction, hatred and tragedy in the world.

There is something in the human mind - something God created - that distinguishes good from bad. Most of us gravitate towards and yearn for all that is good, and we despise what is bad and hateful. We are a part of God's creation with our natural preference for good. The fact is that in our lives, and indeed in creation generally, stuff happens. It does not happen in categories of goodness, indifference and badness. It just happens, and it is we humans who categorise it. And most (granted, not all) "bad" people are equally aware of the categories. The fact that we tend to gravitate towards goodness, or at least yearn for it as a preference, suggests that the urge, the spirit, the principle at work in God, is one of goodness.

It is this spirit, this atmosphere, this urge towards goodness that is the atmosphere in which we prefer to live, and the principle upon which we prefer to base our lives. It is the Holy Spirit. This Spirit is at large in all of creation. This Spirit of the love that is God continues to move upon the face of the waters, and of the land, indeed throughout all that has been created, including each one of us. This Spirit is without and within us, in the very fibres of our being. In the holy space of one of those cathedrals or quiet country churches you can often quite easily sense the Spirit's presence. The very air vibrates with it. But in the daily round of busy life it is not so simple. In all the busyness we easily fail to look out for the Spirit's presence, we miss the Spirit's touch and we miss the Spirit's power to sustain and to transform.

The Island is a great TV reality show. Essentially, a bunch of people are marooned on an uninhabited island in the middle of the Pacific and left to get on with it for a month. At the end of the month they are rescued and taken back to civilization. Whatever happens on that island, they *will* get off it and be taken home eventually.

Now, imagine that in some hidden corner of the island there is a stream of fresh running water and some lovely fruit trees. The castaways haven't found them, but they are pretty sure that they are there somewhere. They have a choice. They could ignore the possibility and live for a month in great discomfort and near starvation and dehydration until they are rescued and taken home, exhausted, ill and remembering their island experience as a really hard and grim one. Or they could go searching, and when they find the fresh stream and fruit they could drink and eat all they need not only to survive, but to thrive, so that the island experience is good and exhilarating. They too will be rescued and taken home at the end of the month, but this time, victorious and having enjoyed the island experience to the full. Now, why on earth wouldn't they choose to go for the stream of life-giving goodness and for the energy-giving fruit? I would, wouldn't you?

God's Spirit is one of affirmation. In the knowledge of the Spirit's presence within and all around us we are more able to sense that we are valuable, unique, special, worthy, loveable, loved and affirmed. Such a Spirit is worth harnessing, invoking and meditating upon. We can come into an awareness and an appreciation of the Spirit of God by all sorts of means: meditation, contemplation, prayer, dedication, commitment and even willpower. We can choose to live in the stream of goodness and in the life-giving energy which is the Holy Spirit.

The Christian life is sometimes hard, just like life on that island is hard, but how much better it is with the fruit; how much better life is with the affirming, sustaining and empowering work of the Holy Spirit. How much better life is, not perfect, but as good as it can possibly be – a taste of God's Kingdom on earth, in this life; and a glimpse, a foretaste of His Kingdom in all its fullness in the next.

I speak of the Holy Spirit as a "stream of goodness". This idea of God's power being displayed and dispensed by means of flowing water is a biblical metaphor. This imagery is repeated time and time again in the Bible.

God is our creator, and there is something in the human heart that yearns for him, that seeks communion with him – the Love that is God. The Psalmist expresses it like this:

As a deer longs for flowing streams,

so my soul longs for you, O God.

My soul thirsts for God,

for the living God. [64]

We journey through life experiencing the tremendous joys and beauty, and the struggles, of simply being alive, but we travel the journey with a sense of yearning, of searching, of wondering in our souls: what's it all about? In the Psalm the deer runs through woods, perhaps pursued by wild animals and, exhausted, it eventually finds a flowing stream from which to drink. The deer is refreshed and restored, ready for the onward journey.

In the Old Testament book of Ezekiel there is the wonderful picture of a stream flowing from the Temple. As it flows away it increases in size and depth. The passage continues:

This water flows towards the eastern region and goes down into the Arabah; and when it enters the sea, the sea of stagnant waters, the water will become fresh. Wherever the river goes, every living creature that swarms will live, and there will be very many fish, once these waters reach there. It will become fresh; and everything will live where the river goes. [65]

This is a lovely picture of the Holy Spirit. In the stream of the Spirit there is refreshment, power and life. If we see the Holy Spirit as the ever present stream of God's creative and loving energy flowing throughout existence, we can choose at least to acknowledge it's presence, and better still, consciously to place ourselves in the stream; if you like, to "go with the flow!" We cannot push the stream or make the stream happen; it is already happening, and we cannot stop it. All we can do is recognize it, enjoy it, and ever more fully allow it to carry us. The flow doesn't have anything to do with us being perfect, right, belonging to the right group, or even understanding the flow. Jesus never had any such checklist test before he healed someone. He just asked, as it were, 'Are you going to ask for or allow yourself to be touched? If so, let's go!'

In most churches these days folk are baptised in still water – either in a font or in a baptistry. Some people however, are baptised in the sea. Imagine: the crashing of the waves, the ceaseless life and energy of the water overwhelming the candidate as a very visceral sign of the life-giving power and energy of the Holy Spirit. In the New Testament there are accounts of baptisms happening in rivers. Jesus himself was baptised by submersion in a river. The symbolism is striking. The river flows with power and energy and the candidate literally places himself in the flow.

Jesus himself spoke of the energizing, sustaining and life-giving Spirit as water. Jesus arrived at Jacob's well after a tiring journey.

A Samaritan woman came to draw water, and Jesus said to her, 'Give me a drink'. (His disciples had gone to the city to buy food.) The Samaritan woman said to him, 'How is it that you, a Jew, ask a drink of me, a woman of Samaria?' (Jews do not share things in common with Samaritans.) Jesus answered her, 'If you knew the gift of God, and who it is that is saying to you, "Give me a drink", you would have asked him, and he would have given you living water.' The woman said to him, 'Sir, you have no bucket, and the well is deep. Where do you get that living water? Are you greater than our ancestor Jacob, who gave us the well, and with his sons and his flocks drank from it?' Jesus said to her, 'Everyone who drinks of this water will be thirsty again, but those who drink of the water that I will give them will never be thirsty. The water that I will give will become in them a spring of water gushing up to eternal life.' The woman said to him, 'Sir, give me this water, so that I may never be thirsty or have to keep coming here to draw water.' [66]

What a powerful image: 'The water that I will give will become in them a spring of water gushing up to eternal life.'

The Holy Spirit is the transformative essence, energy, presence and power of God in all of creation – always there and always everywhere for us to choose to acknowledge; for us to choose consciously to tap into. In some kinds of Christian worship one might hear an invocation of the Holy Spirit along these lines: 'Come, Holy Spirit, fill this place.' However, the Holy Spirit is already filling that place, and every place, and everyone. Surely the invocation might better be: 'Thank you, Holy Spirit, for filling this place. May we open our hearts to you now.'

There is a force for good in the universe and if we align ourselves with and immerse ourselves in this force, we are carried onward to life in all its fullness in the here and now and into eternity. We will be in the stream of goodness, carried along by everything that is right. This is the atmosphere in which we prefer to live; it is the principle upon which we prefer to base our lives. Jesus Christ lived a life submerged in that stream of goodness. He is our model whom we worship, follow, aspire to be like, and whom we place at the centre of our lives.

This stream of goodness, which is the Holy Spirit, is powerful. One who is living in the knowledge and appreciation of the ever present Holy Spirit is one who is empowered by the loving goodness which is the Spirit's very essence. Such a force, when given our leave to be at work in our lives, is empowering and enabling; such a force is affirming and equipping; such a force is enlightening and inspiring. We can choose to live in the stream of goodness, of God-ness. We can choose to live in *the glory of power*.

Chapter Six

Look Well To This Day

One of the key pillars of the twelve step programme for recovering alcoholics (and other kinds of addicts) is "keep it in the day", or "just for today". This simple rule of life is transformative for millions of addicts all over the world as they, day by day and one day at a time, maintain their sobriety and enjoy a life free from slavery to the addictive substance and the addictive mind. Those in the programme who live by this simple rule of life often come to enjoy a long and content life – life in all its fullness.

The thought for an alcoholic of never ever taking a drink for the rest of their life can be a daunting, even frightening, and almost impossible prospect: 'How on earth will I cope when times are really tough, when a loved one dies, when my job is especially stressful, when there are celebrations – weddings, birthdays, anniversaries, Christmas? How on earth will I cope without a drink?'

However, if the addict determines not to worry about those future events, not to live them in their mind before they happen; if the addict resolves only to stay sober for today and to turn their attention to tomorrow when tomorrow comes, then the prospect is much easier: 'All I have to do is not drink today. I may or may not drink tomorrow. I am not even thinking about whether I will drink tomorrow. I am only concerned with not drinking today.' Each day thus begun, is another day of sobriety, freedom and life as good as it can be in their particular circumstances. Each day is life in all its fullness. And the days stack up into weeks, months and years – a life of freedom from bondage to destructive substances and behaviours, a life lived in relative contentment and peace. This is a mindful way of living.

In the fast-paced, highly competitive culture of 21st century western life, the meditative practice of Mindfulness has become widely practiced by people of all faiths and of none. The core principle is the same, but is narrowed down not to "the day", but to "the moment". Spending some time each day emptying the mind of all that has gone before and all that is to come, and consciously being in the very moment, is restorative and refreshing and, for many, very necessary. The practice of such a discipline enables one to practice it in the challenging and stressful experiences that come our way so that we can all the better manage them, coming through mentally and spiritually in tact and able to enjoy life's journey.

This way of life – *looking well to this day* – is a way spoken about and encouraged by Jesus. Of course the past is to be remembered, and where it has been good, to be rejoiced in. But a dwelling on the past which embitters us, which angers us, or which we continually allow to disgrace us, is a kind of slavery. We are held in that place and our present is marred and disfigured by it. The future too is to be considered and often planned for. Not to do so would be unwise, foolish and irresponsible. But a dwelling on the future which worries us, which frightens us, or which we continually allow to threaten us, is also a kind of slavery. Likewise, we are held in that imagined future place and our present is marred and disfigured by it.

Jesus said:

'Therefore I tell you, do not worry about your life, what you will eat or what you will drink, or about your body, what you will wear. Is not life more than food, and the body more than clothing? Look at the birds of the air; they neither sow nor reap nor gather into barns, and yet your heavenly Father feeds them. Are you not of more value than they? And can any of you by worrying add a single hour to your span of

*life? And why do you worry about clothing?
Consider the lilies of the field, how they
grow; they neither toil nor spin, yet I tell
you, even Solomon in all his glory was not
clothed like one of these. But if God so
clothes the grass of the field, which is alive
today and tomorrow is thrown into the oven,
will he not much more clothe you - you of
little faith? Therefore do not worry, saying,
"What will we eat?" or "What will we
drink?" or "What will we wear?" For it is
the Gentiles who strive for all these things;
and indeed your heavenly Father knows that
you need all these things. But strive first for
the kingdom of God and his righteousness,
and all these things will be given to you as
well. 'So do not worry about tomorrow, for
tomorrow will bring worries of its own.
Today's trouble is enough for today.'* [67]

Jesus is encouraging mindful living, keeping it in the
day. His words are a powerful reminder of the *bliss of growth:*
God's extraordinary provision in all he has created and for all

he has created.   Today well lived is a firm foundation for tomorrow.

Jesus is encouraging the *splendour of action:* "striving first for the Kingdom of God". This is a life lived, today, following in the way of Jesus which is the way of *agape* love. For as we have already seen, such a life promotes unity, peace, joy, contentment, enough of what we need – the Kingdom of God.

Jesus is encouraging a life lived, today, attuned to the *glory of power:* a life lived in the stream of goodness which is the very nature of the Holy Spirit and which is at large throughout creation.

We can look to the past, to our Christian inheritance brought to us through the scriptures - the story of people's encounters with God and their understanding of him. We can look to the future with joyful hope, full of encouragement and promise mediated to us in the life and death of Jesus, and the refusal of Love to die. But all we have right now is right now. All we have is this day. Every day lived with a commitment to this day, with a desire to live this day following in the way of Jesus, in the way of Love, and with our minds and hearts open to the Spirit - attuned to the ever flowing stream of the Spirit, is a life well-lived, is to know life in all its fullness; for *today well lived makes every yesterday a dream of happiness and every tomorrow a vision of hope. Look well, therefore, to this day.*

--Notes--

[1] Sanskrit proverb by Kalidasa, Indian poet and playwright, fifth century A.D.

[2] An evangelistic course which seeks to introduce the basics of the Christian faith through a series of talks and discussions. See http://alpha.org/

[3] A kind of apprenticeship for vicars.

[4] A Hindu religious teacher; used as a title of respect

[5] Taken from *Undersong*, by Peter Price, published and copyright © 2002 by Darton Longman and Todd Ltd, London, and used by permission of the publishers, pages 100-102.

[6] The small and underdeveloped island community in South East India which had become my brother's workplace and second home.

[7] Name changed

[8] John 11:32, NRSV

[9] 1 John 4:8, 1 John 4:16

[10] Luke 15

[11] John 11:33-35

[12] Roman 8:38-39, NRSV

[13] Luke 15:24, NRSV

[14] Psalm 44:24-27, Grail Version. Have a look at the whole Psalm.

[15] Genesis 1:1, NRSV

[16] Genesis 22:1-2, NRSV

[17] Deuteronomy 20:16-18, NRSV

[18] 1 Samuel 18:10, NRSV

[19] John 4:24, NRSV

[20] Genesis 1:4,10, 12,18,21,25,31, NRSV

[21] Genesis 1:27-28, NRSV

[22] Genesis 1:31, NRSV

[23] Isaiah 40:30-31, NRSV

[24] 1 John 4:16, NRSV

[25] John 2:1-11

[26] Matthew 14:13-21, Mark 6:30-44, Luke 9:10-17, John 6:1-15

[27] Matthew 9:10-13, Mark 2:15-17, Luke 5:29-32

[28] Luke 11:37ff

[29] Luke 14:1-24

[30] Matthew 26:26-30, Mark 14:22-25, Luke 22:14-38, John 13:1ff

[31] John 2:1-12

[32] Luke 15-23

[33] Luke 14:8

[34] Luke 14:15-24
[35] Luke 11:5-8
[36] Matthew 15:32
[37] 1 John 4:8, 1 John 4:16
[38] 1 John 4:8, 1 John 4:16
[39] John 13:34-35, NRSV
[40] Matthew 22:37-40, NRSV; and see Mark 12:30-31, Luke 10:27
[41] *Agape* in the original Greek
[42] Luke 6:27-30 NRSV; see also Matthew 5:43-44
[43] Mark 5
[44] Mark 5:4
[45] Mark 5:15-17
[46] Leviticus 15.19-25, NRSV
[47] Mark 5:25-34, Matthew 9:20-22, Luke 8 ;43-48
[48] Mark 5:34, NRSV
[49] Exodus 20:14, NRSV
[50] Leviticus 20:10, NRSV
[51] Deuteronomy 22:22, NRSV
[52] John 8:11, NRSV
[53] Luke 7:36-50
[54] Luke 23:34, NRSV
[55] Acts 24:14
[56] Matthew 16:24, Mark 8:34, Luke 9:23
[57] Matthew 22:37-40, Mark 12:30-31, Luke 10:27
[58] From the day he was sworn into office (April 22, 2003) as leader of the Ahmadiyya Muslim Community, he has committed himself to extending a message of peace to the world, he exhorts Muslims worldwide to strengthen interfaith relationships, and he champions religious freedom.
[59] Luke 23:34
[60] Luke 23:43
[61] 1 John 4:8, 1 John 4:16
[62] John 4:24
[63] Genesis 1:1-2, NRSV
[64] Psalm 42:1-2 NRSV
[65] Ezekiel 47:8-9 NRSV
[66] John 4:7-15 NRSV
[67] Matthew 6:25-34 NRSV

38901062R00050

Printed in Great Britain
by Amazon